Beyond

— the —

Boardroom

by
Deeawn Roundtree

"Beyond the Boardroom," by Deeawn Roundtree. ISBN 1-58939-821-1.

Published 2005 by Virtualbookworm.com Publishing Inc., P.O. Box 9949, College Station, TX 77842, US. ©2005, Deeawn Roundtree.

Manufactured in the United States of America.

Table of Contents

In Appreciation:

To my Lord and Savior, Jesus Christ: Apart from You, I can do nothing. You have blessed me beyond measure. Thank You.

To my husband, Ray: Thank you for your supportive love and strength. Your friendship and wisdom have truly blessed me.

To my son, Matthew, God's perfect gift: Because of you, I am inspired to reach my full potential and to make you the happiest child alive.

To my mentor, Estella: Your strength of character, honesty and forthrightness will always be cherished.

Lastly, to my family and friends who have challenged, loved and supported me throughout my life: May the Lord bless and keep you.

*"Beyond the Boardroom" is dedicated to the
precious memory of my grandmother,
Sally Hendricks,
whose undying love strengthens me each day.*

Introduction:
Beyond the Boardroom

When I graduated from high school I knew I would have to get a job before thinking about going to college. My plan was to get hired by a company that would help to pay for my college education, and that is eventually what I did. My first job out of high school was as a teller for a major bank in the city. I was a part-time bank teller in a teller-pool, which meant that I went from branch to branch, wherever I was needed to fill-in. What I liked most about the job was that I got to meet new people each day, however, no one got to know me too well, and therefore, they did not get a chance to form a negative opinion about me. It was enjoyable. Then I was offered a permanent teller position that I gladly accepted. This started my learning process in corporate America. During my employment with the bank, I learned fast that working with people was still like being in high school. Some people are extremely competitive, some confrontational and some are deceitful. They smile in your face and talk behind your back. It was hard to accept this at first. I thought that once I started working for money, I would not have to deal with the pettiness that every high school student deals with because now

1

I was working with "adults." However, corporate America is no different from high school except that you cannot threaten to beat a person up after work for talking about you or conduct yourself unprofessionally without hurting yourself, your career, getting fired or maybe even sued. Many days during my corporate work experience my feelings were hurt, I felt anger, disappointment and confusion, wondering why some people did not like me.

I was not prepared for the corporate environment. There wasn't anyone that I could talk to about this. When I tried talking to people about what I was feeling, they seemed to be feeling the same way that I was. Had I known then what I know now, I would have been a much happier and a more successful employee. Getting through the interview process is just the beginning to succeeding in the corporate environment. This book is written to help people better understand the "game" that they must learn to play in order to be successful and happy in their work environment.

During my 20 years of work experience in corporate America, I learned the hard way that just being myself in the corporate environment would not make me successful or happy. Being myself meant to be honest about what I thought and felt and expressing those thoughts and feelings whenever it was appropriate. Being myself meant that I tried to make friends with the people I worked with by sharing my experiences with them as they shared their experiences with me. Being myself meant that I trusted those who seemed to like me.

Deeawn Roundtree

Being myself meant that whenever I had a problem with a fellow co-worker, I would work it out with them, one-on-one. How wrong I was to think that being myself was the way to succeed in corporate America.

Corporate America plays by a different set of rules. Unfortunately, if you don't know what those rules are, you will be left feeling bewildered, confused, discouraged, unhappy and disappointed. It took a while for me to learn the game, to play the game, and then to win in spite of the game, but I did. Now, I realize that many people come into corporate America as unprepared as I was. Also, there are those who have worked in corporate America for many years that are unhappy because they still do not understand the rules of the game, much less know how to play it.

Let's start by describing what the "game" is. The "game" is a set of unspoken rules that one must follow in order to make people in the corporate environment feel comfortable with you and to like you. It is learning how to communicate with others with such diplomacy that you *never* offend those in authority or your peers. It is gaining favor with your bosses and peers so that even when you do make a mistake, it is quickly over-looked, minimized or excused. It is understanding that whether you are promoted or not is subjective to those who are the decision makers. This is based on whether or not they think you fit into the corporate culture and if you are worthy of promotion. It is learning what makes those in authority happy and saying what they want to hear. It is overall conducting yourself in such a way that "they" approve of you.

I first entered corporate America at the age of 18 years old. It wasn't until I became a sales representative at the age of 31, that I learned how to play the game well enough to succeed in spite of the conspicuous nature of office politics that were played. In the sales industry, men and women can be phony, ruthless and selfish. Most are only thinking about themselves and how they are perceived or how to get recognized.

I learned the hard way that the perception that others have of you can either hinder or help your career. However, as a sales professional, you may have the ability to succeed in spite of what others think because of your performance, which is mostly measured by sales. Yet, if you desire to be promoted, your sales performance alone will not be enough.

Managing the perception that others have of you comes down to understanding what your boss and co-workers think about you. If you are unsure, ask them how you come across when you speak or by the way that you carry yourself. Hopefully, you will receive honest feedback.

Sometimes people are perceived as aggressive, confrontational, possessing a negative attitude, angry, emotional or defensive. Sometimes this is true because many of us carry baggage from our past employers, childhood experiences, past relationships, current relationships and bad experiences overall that we end up creating a negative perception for ourselves.

Deeawn Roundtree

How can you manage the perception others have of you in corporate America? **One**, dress like those in management, whether it's conservative or trendy. **Two**, keep a low profile and never gossip about others in the workplace. **Three**, never speak negatively about your co-workers to your boss. **Four**, never speak negatively about your boss to your co-workers. **Five**, keep your personal life and personal business to yourself. **Six**, do not discuss religion, sex or politics at work. **Seven,** choose a mentor who can make a positive difference in your career. **Eight**, do not hang around troublemakers or those who have bad reputations. **Nine,** do not share your career or company ideas with anyone unless you trust them and you have them written down. **Ten**, do not confront someone if they offend you at work. **Eleven**, do not be a know-it-all or arrogant. **Twelve**, go the extra mile, and when you do keep a record in order to remember for your annual performance review. **Thirteen**, do not make personal phone calls at work where others can hear your conversation. **Fourteen**, do not use your company computer to check personal e-mails or for personal use and be professional when writing business-related e-mails. **Fifteen**, take ownership and responsibility for your career and actively pursue your career goals. **Sixteen**, make sure you know who the decision makers are in your company. **Seventeen**, do not cry at work. **Eighteen**, be diplomatic during business meetings. **Nineteen**, do not be a brownnoser. **Twenty**, learn business-dining etiquette. **Twenty-one**, be smart about dating in the workplace. **Twenty-two**, be a trusted team-player. **Twenty-three**, develop excellent customer service skills. **Twenty-four**, avoid touching in the workplace. **Twenty-five**, try not to burn bridges when you leave a company.

In the following chapters, I will share with you what I learned during my career and discuss the many mistakes that people make in corporate America so that you will avoid making the same ones yourself.

Chapter 1:
Dress like management

Your dress should reflect the corporate culture. It is necessary that our outward appearance reflects a positive image of us. That means that if management is conservative you need to dress conservatively or if they dress trendy or casual, you should dress more trendy or business casual. Also, make sure you understand what your company's definition of business casual dress is.

When I first started in the sales industry, I had to go to out of town for training. Prior to joining the sales industry, I worked for a utility company whose dress was somewhat business casual. Their definition of business casual, however, was more like weekend casual, because some people wore jeans and warm-up suits. So when I was told that the attire for the sales training would be business casual, I purchased two silk warm up suits with matching blouses and shoes. For the first day of training, I decided to play it safe and wear the nicest outfit I brought which was a charcoal blue, two-piece skirt suit. I am so glad that I did. When

I attended training, the women looked like they stepped out of a Vogue magazine. They looked like fashion models who shopped at Saks Fifth Avenue, Lord & Taylor and Neiman Marcus. Although I was dressed appropriately for that day, I was embarrassed just thinking about what I had to wear for the rest of the week. Fortunately, I had a credit card with a zero balance. After training that day, I went shopping for several new appropriate business casual outfits. Needless to say, I never wore those silk warm-up suits to work. I learned that every industry has it own definition of what business casual dress is. That is not to say that you should be over-dressed. This too could draw unwanted and negative attention. You may even come across as thinking you are better than others or that you want undue attention. It is better to dress more understated than flashy. For example, a young lady whom I worked closely with loved to wear her expensive jewelry and flamboyant dress suits. However, instead of getting the compliments she desired, others talked about her behind her back and wondered what she was trying to prove. The same goes for hairstyles. Depending on the industry, your hair should reflect the corporate culture. Braids may be fine for a very casual workplace, your own business or the fashion industry. However, they may not be appropriate for the banking, pharmaceutical or computer industry. Understanding your corporate culture is key.

I remember when I wore my hair naturally curly for a national meeting at the home office of our company, and a fellow co-worker remarked to someone else behind my back that she did not think natural curls were business-like. The person who said this did not have any authority, however, she had a lot of influence in the workplace. Therefore, although it was only her opinion, her perception of me could have a negative impact on my career if she shared her opinion with others. No, I did not agree with her at the time, nor did I like her opinion. But, perception is everything in business. Inasmuch as, she had more influence and experience in the industry than I had, I heeded what she said.

Chapter 2:
Keep a low profile and never gossip about others because it will get back to them

Let your work speak for itself. You do not have to be a show-off or be a loud mouth in order to get noticed. I remember working with a woman who was about 15 years older than me. Everyone showed an enormous amount of respect for her even though she was not in a managerial position. She kept to herself and you never heard her or saw her gossiping or speaking negatively about others. She never gave her opinion and worked impeccably. Eventually, she was promoted to a management position because of her low profile, yet excellent work ethic. There was another woman, however, whom I worked with who made a fuss about everything she did. She had a reputation for being a trouble-maker and was disliked by most people who knew her or worked with her. When she was over-looked for promotion because of her negative attitude, she decided to sue the company for discrimination.

Beyond the Boardroom

A person who gossips about others can never be trusted. You never know if they are gossiping about you the same way that they gossip to you about others. Not only that, this kind of behavior is very unprofessional in the workplace. It normally comes back to haunt the person who gossips, and they may never recover from the words they spoke.

Also, gossipers are normally people who feel insecure about themselves and who are not going anywhere in their careers. They think that by putting others down, it will elevate who they are in the eyes of others. Yet, what it does is just the opposite because by fostering a negative work environment, they create a negative image of themselves.

Chapter 3:
Never speak negatively about your co-workers to your boss

Sometimes bosses will try to get their employees to confide in them about their fellow co-workers. Because the employee wants to get in good with the boss, they may share their true feelings even if they are negative. They believe this may help them in their relationship with the boss, particularly if they know the boss doesn't like the person. More often than not, this will definitely backfire should you make a mistake one day and get on your boss's bad side. I remember working for this type of person. He would ask me questions about other people in the workplace to see what I thought. Being the honest, naïve person that I was, I would speak freely thinking it might strengthen my relationship with my boss. It turned out that my boss asked questions of everyone who worked for him. He used our very words against us to his advantage. He promoted his favorite individuals, and did not promote those he did not like. It was a sneaky, but effective way to keep everyone suspicious of each other and competitive. If the majority of the department had a negative opinion about one person in the department, he used this to keep that person from being promoted, despite their performance.

If your boss asks you what you think about your co-workers, give vague, neutral answers. Never say anything that may incriminate you in the future. If it is someone you dislike, keep your thoughts and feelings to yourself. If you need to discuss this person's behavior, speak to someone outside the company or discuss it with a mentor. If you are having a severe problem with a co-worker, and you cannot work it out between yourselves, it may be necessary to meet with Human Resources. However, be sure that your company's Human Resources department is fair and unbiased. In my experience, some Human Resources departments are geared to look out for management only. In that case, you may need to seek outside counsel for further assistance.

Chapter 4:
Never speak negatively about your boss to your co-workers

We all do this or are tempted to do this out of frustration and anger. However, may I suggest that instead of venting to your co-workers about the behavior of your boss, whom you will have to work with on a regular basis, talk to a friend, spouse, family member or mentor and vent to them. The fact is that if you get on your co-workers' bad side one day, co-workers may share the details of your conversation. In addition, if you and your co-workers compete for promotion, your co-workers may sabotage your career by trying to make you look bad by repeating to your boss your negative comments. Instead of regretting what you said to your co-workers about your boss, vent to someone outside of work.

I remember confiding in a co-worker about a particular boss that I did not like and was having problems with. My co-worker shared what I said with the boss and from then on my boss did not treat me favorably. How I wished I had not made that mistake, but it was a good lesson learned. Now, when co-workers come around me and start bad-mouthing the boss or fellow co-workers, I have learned to listen and remain neutral. In remaining neutral or silent, you may be perceived as a prude, but you will be wiser and better off in the end. If you must give an opinion because you are asked directly, give an unbiased and/or a positive response.

Chapter 5:
Keep your personal life and personal business to yourself

I realize this is difficult to do, especially when others are sharing their personal lives with you. However, in the business environment this is not appropriate. Remember, perception is everything and a negative one is created by other's opinion of you whether it is right or wrong. In order to avoid negative judgments, the less your co-workers know about you personally, the less they will have to use against you.

Some bosses have a way of trying to get to know you by gaining your trust and making you feel comfortable enough with them that you begin to answer personal questions about your life, such as relationships, political and/or religious preferences. However, avoid answering these questions like the plague. For example, previous bosses would ask my opinion about particular lifestyle choices. Because I did not always agree with them, this later was used to prevent me from being promoted. I highly recommend that you never share your true thoughts or feelings about personal topics or controversial issues, especially if you think it could be used against you later. Instead give neutral responses in order to protect your reputation and the perception others will have of you.

Chapter 6:
Do not discuss religion, sex or politics at work

Discussing topics of religion, sex or politics is not appropriate for the workplace. It will give others the chance to judge you and even hold something against you if your views and beliefs are different from your boss or co-workers. Again, if a co-worker or boss brings up these subjects to you, listen, but remain neutral. Instead allow your actions and lifestyle to speak for you. The way that you treat others in the workplace and how you carry yourself will speak volumes about who you are as a person. Also, keep in mind that no one is perfect. Therefore, if you go around trying to convert others to your way of thinking, you set yourself up to be accused of feeling superior. If, and when you have a bad day at work and it shows in your actions, others may judge you and accuse you of being a hypocrite, especially if your actions are unpleasant and contradictory to what you've preached to others. Also, your boss may accuse you of wasting company time and thinking that you have a poor work ethic. Schedule to meet with the individual after work hours if they want to further discuss what you believe.

In my early years of working in corporate America, I used to tell others about my faith and sometimes I would get over-zealous and end up in controversial discussions. Needless to say, I turned off my co-workers. I learned that the best way for me to represent what I believe is to let others witness my lifestyle and my actions. Now, I try to work hard, be kind, forgiving and understanding, and go the extra mile. Then if someone wants to speak to me because they admire my work ethic and personality, I am able to share with them what governs my life.

Also, some people feel comfortable sharing intimate details about their sex life. Again, I highly recommend that you avoid this subject in the workplace. It will be very easy for you to create a negative perception of yourself and also make others uncomfortable with you.

Chapter 7:
Choose a mentor who can make a positive difference in your career

Having a mentor has been a gift to me since I started working. I chose a person whom I respected, admired and wanted to emulate. This person was also in an executive management position and was well liked and respected by others in the company. She is a very forthright and direct individual. She never sugar coats anything. I knew exactly what she meant when she gave me sound business advice about how to handle particular situations that would arise in the workplace. Even after I left the company that we both worked for, I still kept her for my mentor and my relationship with her helped me in other companies I was employed by. Because I know my mentor so well, many times I did not have to contact her directly to discuss a situation. I would simply do what I knew she would advise me to do.

In a mentoring relationship, most of the time you should and will be the initiator. Normally, mentors are very busy people and therefore, they may not have time to track you down. Since you are the one who is benefiting most from the relationship, don't hesitate to contact them. Normally, the mentor will appreciate your admiration and the opportunity to assist you in your career goals, because it is their way of giving back. Offer to take your potential mentor out to lunch and of course, pay for it. Explain to them why you want and need a mentor and why you hope he or she will agree. Never waste your mentor's time and don't whine or blame others for your unhappiness at work. Be honest in your dialogue and take responsibility for any mistakes that you make in the workplace. Your mistakes will be great learning tools for you and your mentor to discuss and will allow your mentor to give you relevant feedback.

You may decide to choose more than one mentor. You may choose one for your business and career life and one for your personal life. As long as you are both comfortable with the relationship and you can trust your mentor, this is what's most important.

Chapter 8:
Do not hang around troublemakers or those who have bad reputations

There is a saying that goes, "Birds of a feather flock together." Others will judge you by the company you keep in business. You may think that this is unfair, but it is true. That is not to say that you should be rude to people, however, you do not want to attach yourself to someone who is perceived negatively. Again, neutrality is the key in order to protect your reputation. Be nice and kind to everyone. Smile and try to participate in company activities. Get to know different people. If you decide to hang around one particular person, choose someone who is viewed positively throughout the company and who is on the fast track. This is particularly important if you desire to get promoted or hired by another company. If you decide to tell an interviewer that you know a particular person who works for the company, make sure you know that the reputation of the person is positive. If you share the name of an individual who has a bad reputation, it may hinder your chances for promotion or for a new job. If the interviewer has a negative perception of the individual you named, you may not get the job.

Chapter 9:

Do not share your career or company ideas with anyone unless you trust them and you have them written down

This may seem obvious, however, I can remember many times when I shared an idea that would improve the way our company or department functioned and sure enough, that someone took credit for the idea during a meeting. So, before sharing your great idea write it down, submit it to your boss or share it openly during a meeting at an appropriate time. If you choose to share your ideas during a meeting, be sure there are other key witnesses present, such as upper management, especially if you do not trust your direct supervisor or your fellow co-workers. Also, if you happen to be on the receiving end and a co-worker shares a great idea with you, don't take credit for it. If that person is afraid to share their idea, ask them for permission to share it and if they agree, be sure to give credit to that individual. You never know when he or she will return the favor. It will also make you look credible and trustworthy to others.

Beyond the Boardroom

We will discuss further how to conduct yourself during business meetings in Chapter 18.

Chapter 10:
Do not confront someone if they offend you at work

Not confronting someone who offends you may go against everything you believe or were taught as a child. However, in business I have learned the hard way that it is in your best interest and for your career enhancement to avoid confrontation even when offended. Although everything within you wants to speak to that person about the situation, show self-control and restraint. You will only regret confronting that person later. **Think about the situation thoroughly and ask yourself these questions:** 1.) How important is this situation in the larger scheme of things? 2.) Is the person worth the effort and energy? 3.) Can they make a difference in your career? 4.) If the person responds negatively, how much would confronting them escalate the situation? Instead of confronting the person, walk away, discuss the situation with someone you trust and resolve it within yourself first. **If the other person decides to confront you**, 1.) Be sure you are alone, just the two of you

27

or bring someone who is neutral as a witness. If there are company people around schedule a different place and time for you to meet. 2.) Keep your emotions in check, especially if the other person becomes belligerent or defensive. Walk away before getting caught up in the fray. 3.) Discuss the situation over a meal preferably in a restaurant away from work. 4.) If necessary, agree to disagree. It is more important to make peace, than to be right.

Chapter 11:

Do not be a know-it-all or arrogant

A sure way to damage your career in any company is to come across as being a know-it-all
and arrogant. If you don't offend your boss or co-
workers, you may end up offending your company's clients. Normally, you want to remain
teachable and humble in your relationship with
others in the company and outside. Always be
open to learn new techniques, skills and ideas.
Even if you think you know-it-all restrain yourself
from showing it. Many times I have gone to a client's office and a manager or a staff person is discussing how a particular sales representative has
an arrogant attitude. The manager and staff are so
turned off by that representative that they will
prevent the individual from speaking with their
boss to try to sell their product. The manager and
staff will simply use a competitor's product instead.

Chapter 12:
Go the extra mile, and when you do, keep a record in order to remember for your annual performance review

Set yourself apart from your co-workers within the company, as well as from the competition from other companies. Your clients will remember how different you are from other vendors and your boss will see you more favorably than your co-workers. No matter how much you believe your boss will remember your efforts, keep a record of your accomplishments throughout the year. This will help you during your annual performance reviews. Many times bosses are unaware of all you do to contribute above and beyond your job description. Then they wonder why you do not agree with their assessment of you or with the performance rating you receive. This has happened to me on several occasions and because I kept good records, my performance rating was changed to a better one. Also, going the extra mile will help you when you change companies or careers even if you are not able to receive a good reference from your present employer. If you have delivered exceptional service and developed positive relationships with your former clients, you may be able to ask them to write a letter of recommendation for you. However, if you do leave on favorable terms, your boss will remember your hard work and how you distinguished yourself from others.

Chapter 13:
Do not make personal phone calls at work, especially when others can hear your conversation

I am sure many of you have gone to a place of business and over-heard the personal conversations of the receptionist discussing a date or clearly having some other personal conversation. This is totally unprofessional and makes a negative impression of you and your company. Additionally, your co-workers are able to hear your personal business, which could later be used against you. Be smart. With the advent of cellular phones, you may make personal phone calls on your coffee or lunch break in a private place, thereby, protecting your reputation and that of your company's. Always acknowledge those who come to your desk by making eye contact and signaling that you will be with them in a moment.

If you are on a personal call, discontinue your conversation immediately and proceed to help the person at your desk. If you are on a business call, complete your call and then give your full attention to the person. When you are on the phone and another call comes in, let the new caller know that you are on another line, but that you will return their call as soon as possible. Speak pleasantly when you are on the phone and smile. This enhances the tone quality of your voice and makes you sound pleasant and professional. If you are answering someone else's phone, be sure to take the message correctly. Also, if you are going to be away from your desk for a while, be sure that your phone goes to voice mail after three to five rings, or designate someone else to answer it.

Chapter 14:

Do not use your company computer to check personal e-mails or for personal use and be professional in business-related e-mails

Again, discretion in business is key. Using your company computer for personal use is dangerous to your career. You never know who has access to company databases, thereby, jeopardizing your reputation and even worse, your career. Also, when using your e-mail for company-related business, do not send derogatory messages about your co-workers or boss. Also, write your e-mails in a memo-style format. Always use a salutation and close your e-mails appropriately. You never know who may end up with your e-mail. In business-related e-mails be concise and professional. E-mails are not to be written like letters. Also, don't waste your co-workers time by passing along jokes or chain e-mails. This is totally unprofessional and will make you look immature and prove that you are wasting company time.

Chapter 15:
Take ownership and responsibility for your career and actively pursue your career goals

It is up to you to take responsibility for reaching your career goals. Do not wait for your boss to notice your hard work or accomplishments. However, make sure your career goals are known by your boss and others in positions to assist you in achieving your goals. Network with others in the company who possess the power to not only recognize who you are, but who can also make decisions on your behalf. I did not realize how important this was until near the end of my career as a sales representative. When I did, I saw a difference immediately. I was registered for various training courses, received assignments that provided more exposure for me and was given additional responsibilities and opportunities. Continue to make your desires known to your immediate supervisor and ask for the opportunity to showcase your talents and skills. If all else fails, discuss your concerns with your boss and even your boss's boss to find out what you can do to get promoted. If there are skills you need to acquire or if management has a legitimate reason for not promoting you, work on gaining those skills or improving your behavior if there is a problem. Once a reasonable period of time has passed and you have consistently demonstrated positive efforts to improve your behavior, and you still believe that you are being passed-over, discuss the situation with Human Resources. If this is not helpful, start looking for other opportunities outside of your company. It is never worth wasting your valuable time and efforts in a company when your best efforts and talents are neither recognized nor appreciated. Sometimes, just realizing that there are other and even better opportunities out there will do wonders for your confidence and self-esteem.

Chapter 16:
Make sure you know who the decision makers are in your company

This may seem obvious by now and we touched on it earlier. However, I can remember working for companies and not knowing and caring enough to know the executive management. For example, I was introduced to the president of a company and when I asked what he did for the company, the person who introduced us said emphatically, "This is the company president!" You can only imagine how I felt and how I looked to the person who has this influence and power, not to mention what affect this could have on my career. Therefore, I strongly advise that when you attend corporate meetings or when you receive an annual report, identify the movers and shakers in the company. Even if you do not know exactly what these individuals look like, you can at least find out who holds various positions, what their names are and what their roles are in the company. This way, when you do have the opportunity to meet these individuals in person, you will know who they are and will be able to have an intelligent conversation. It will also put you in a better position to seek out mentors and introduce yourself to them.

You always want to be able to make a good first impression. It is normally lasting. In the future should your name come up in conversation among management, they may recall your interaction and have a positive opinion of you. Even if the conversation about you happens to be negative for some unknown reason, at least those who met you in person will remember you positively and may even speak up on your behalf.

Chapter 17:
Do not cry at work

Not only is crying at work unprofessional, but it gives the impression that you are a weak individual. I know a young lady who by all accounts was a very sweet and good-hearted person. However, she had a terrible reputation for crying at work. Not only was this apparent among her peers and management, but also by the company's clients. Many times people felt like they had to walk on eggshells. They could not have an adult conversation with her because she was overly sensitive. Shared-clients openly spoke about her conduct in their offices. Therefore, her co-workers were placed in a position to minimize her behavior in order to keep from losing business and credibility. After many conversations with her and finally her own realization, she stopped crying.

If you happen to be an emotional person who cannot take criticism or who wears your feelings on your sleeve, learn to use self-restraint and find someone outside of work with whom you can confide. It is always best to appear professional and in control of yourself at work. Also, everyone has personal baggage that they must carry on a daily basis, yet continue to meet the needs of their employer first. Remember, you are not alone. If your personal situation is so overwhelming, it may be best for you to take a personal day, if you can. It is better not to go to work under such emotional strain, than to damage your career in the process. Lastly, when you cry in front of your co-workers or boss, this may cause them to lose respect for you and to label you as unmanageable. Your boss may also feel that you are not fit for promotion as a result of this behavior. If you do not have thick skin, learn to fake it and after you have taken the critical comments from a co-worker or boss, hold it together until you can find time alone. Keep in mind that it is not the end of the world because you receive a bad performance review, or if someone does not like you. Make sure your life and identity are not wrapped up solely in your career or the company you work for, or the people you work with. Something I have learned for sure, is that you can and will eventually be replaced and probably forgotten once you leave a company. Move on and let negative experiences at work roll off your back. Stay focused on why you are there and what you want to accomplish for you and your family.

Chapter 18:
Be diplomatic during business meetings

B e careful and very tactful about the comments
you make during business meetings. It is important for you to participate constructively. Have
something positive and productive to contribute
and be prepared to ask and answer questions that
may arise. Look alert and pay attention to what is
going on. Do not have sidebar conversations or
make negative comments under your breath. This
is the time for you to shine. The time when the
managerial staff will want to get to know you and
see what you have to contribute to the company.
In the sales industry, this is even more pro-
nounced. Everything you say, your posture, dress,
participation or lack thereof, will be scrutinized
closely. Use the meetings to showcase your talents
and the value that you bring to the company. If
you have a problem that may be perceived as
negative if shared openly during the meeting, always have a solution to back it up. If you do not
have a solution, do not use the meeting as a time

to vent your frustrations and concerns. However, you should meet with your immediate supervisor after the meeting or between breaks to bring up your concerns. Never interrupt anyone who is speaking during a meeting or snub the comment of a fellow co-worker. If you do, it will make you look bad. Also, have your own original thoughts. Do not piggyback off of the comments of another to make your point. It will look like you are taking sides or that you are using someone else's thoughts and ideas to make yourself look good. If someone speaks up and states what you wanted to say, let that person have the floor and get the credit for speaking up. Come up with something else to contribute to the discussion or just let the moment pass. Also, if you bring up a good idea that is not accepted by others who are facilitating the meeting, discuss your idea further with your boss or the facilitator during the break and find out why they did not support your perspective. However, do not use the meeting to defend your comments. Keep in mind, those who are facilitating the meeting have a strict agenda that they want to follow. Therefore, do not go off on tangents or bring up topics that are irrelevant to the subject being discussed. This will only frustrate the facilitator and make you look less professional in the eyes of management. Realize that those who are facilitating the meeting may not see you in the most favorable light and therefore, may not acknowledge your idea. In fact, they may reject every idea you have in an offensive manner during the meeting. In that case, only share your ideas in the presence of those who would acknowledge and accept them. You may want to write your ideas down and present them to someone with whom you have a good relationship with within the company. This is another reason why it is so important to have a mentor. When situations like these occur during your career, having a mentor to discuss them with will give you an outlet and a chance to hear feedback that is unbiased and beneficial. This will also be helpful to your career in the future.

Chapter 19:
Do not be a brownnoser

What is the definition of a brownnoser? A brownnoser is one who shows too great a willingness to serve or obey those in authority. Someone who brownnoses becomes very obvious to management and to their peers. It is an unattractive trait and will cause a person to lose respect and be seen in a disapproving manner by those with whom they work for and with. In some companies this is more evident than in others. Unfortunately, some have been rewarded for this degrading behavior, but ultimately, the person who becomes a brownnoser will jeopardize their career should someone in authority find this behavior offensive. Have the confidence to stand on your own performance and the positive contributions that you make to the company. That is not say, that you should not make every effort to be kind and courteous with those you come in contact with at work, but you should keep it in balance. Do not lose respect for yourself by using unwarranted and excessive flattery.

Beyond the Boardroom

A particular person in my company was known as a brownnoser. During meetings he would reject the positive comments and ideas that others made and always agreed with what management had to say. If a person in management did not agree with the comments made by someone in the meeting, the brownnoser would disagree with them, as well. It became so obvious and obnoxious, that the person was called aside after the meeting to discuss his behavior. This individual honestly thought it would get him promoted and that he would be seen more favorably by management. However, the result was ultimately just the opposite. He transferred to another city within the company to escape the negative consequences.

Chapter 20:
Learn business-dining etiquette

It is vital to your career and self-confidence during business meals to understand basic table manners, including the positioning of dining utensils. If you are not sure, do your homework prior to attending a business meal. Do not wait until you are at the business meal to watch what others do. This will cause you much anxiety and frustration. You can go on the internet, take a course or ask someone who knows what to do. Open your napkin, fold it and place it on your lap as soon as you sit down. Keep in mind that liquids (water, soft drinks, wine) are placed to your right and solids (bread and butter) are placed to your left. Also, when you start eating, choose the utensil farthest from the plate. If you are starting with a salad, a small salad fork will be on your far left-hand side, or if there is an entrée, it will be a dinner fork. If you are starting with soup, a soup spoon will be farthest away from your plate on the right-hand side. When passing the bread, at a round table (do not take) pass the basket it to your right. At a rectangular table help yourself first and then pass to your right. Always ask someone to pass the condiments to you if they are not in front of you. When you leave the table, place the napkin on your chair and turn your fork faced-down if you are not finished eating. If you have completed your meal then place your knife with the cutting side turned inwards and your fork parallel on the plate in a clock-wise position of 10:20.

Before your business meal, make sure you know who is paying for the check ahead of time. If it is you, then make it known prior to ending the meal. Do not wait until after the meal and bicker about who is paying. Make sure your conversation is appropriate, as well. Do not use this as an opportunity to bad-mouth your boss or fellow co-workers. Discuss general topics such as the weather, interests and hobbies. Do not discuss information that is too personal such as sex, politics or religion. Try not to discuss controversial topics. Keep you conversation light, upbeat and positive. You are still being scrutinized and judged by how you carry yourself during this event. Also, it will be helpful to have a general knowledge about wines and have a favorite drink that you order during these meals. If it is a luncheon, do not drink alcohol. If it is dinner, keep the alcohol to a dinner wine and only one glass. I have seen first-hand how individuals embarrass themselves during business meals. As a result of not using discretion when drinking alcohol, irreparable damage was done to their reputations and careers. Also, if you do not

Deeawn Roundtree

drink, you do not need to broadcast it among others. Simply order a soft drink or water.

Chapter 21:
Be smart about dating
in the workplace

Dating in the workplace is quite common, especially since many women work outside the home. However, it can have drastic adverse effects on your career, especially if your relationship becomes public knowledge within the company. Also, should your relationship not work out, this may create an unpleasant working environment for you. You must decide whether or not the individual you are dating is worth the risk. If you decide the person is worth the risk, then keep these tips in mind. 1.) Know your company policy on dating in the workplace. 2.) Be discreet. Don't tell anyone at work about your relationship. 3.) If you work in the same department, consider transferring to a different one. 4.) Communicate upfront about how you want your relationship to work. Discuss what you will do if your relationship does not workout. Discuss the specific boundaries that you want to set during working hours, such as whether or not you will go to lunch together or whether or not you will contact each other during working hours. Until you are engaged and have set a wedding date, it's best to keep a low profile. 5.) Understand that your reputation is on the line. If the relationship ends negatively and the person you were dating handles it badly, they may try to sabotage your career by spreading negative rumors about you or try to get you to the leave the company. 6.) If you decide to get engaged or married, then discuss it first with your boss prior to telling your co-workers. He or she will advise you on company policy and communicate the news with his or her superiors. Once you've gotten a positive response from your supervisor, ask if it will be acceptable to share with co-workers. This will ensure that you stay in compliance with company procedures and your boss will appreciate your professionalism and respect towards him or her and the company. Also, there may be logistical changes that need to be made if you and your fiancé work in the same department. 7.) Good luck and best wishes.

Chapter 22:
Be a trusted team player

Companies today realize that more will be accomplished and it is more lucrative to their bottom-lines when their employees work together. However, being a team-player is more than just working closely with one person or a group of individuals. It is when your attitude and goals are in line with the company you work for, you are easy to get along with, you understand what is important to your boss, how the company operates and you play a key role in helping your company achieve its goals and objectives. Being a team player is understanding that your behavior at work and away from work reflects on the company you are employed by. It is demonstrating a lifestyle of integrity that is above reproach by your co-workers, clients and management. To be a better team player, get a broader perspective about why your company is in business. Discover innovative ways to help your company and co-workers become more productive. This will make you more valuable to the company and cause you to stand out among your co-workers. Also, learn what is important to your immediate supervisor. Assist him or her whenever possible and take the initiative. However, don't be over zealous in your efforts because you may come across as a "yes-person" or a brownnoser. Just make your boss aware that you are willing to assist whenever possible. Ask for additional responsibility and look for ways to make your boss look good. This will pay off for you in the end and put you in the forefront of his or her mind when it's time to make promotions. Last, but not least, don't forget to document your contributions so that you can remind your boss of how you went the extra-mile when he or she does your performance review. Whenever you are working on a project that requires a team effort, find out what your role will be. Communicate constantly and clearly with one another. Meet on a regular basis to go over your progress and to make sure that everyone is still on the same page. If and when a conflict arises, choose a neutral party to be a mediator if you are unable to work it out yourself. If that doesn't work, as a last resort, discuss the problem with your immediate supervisor, indicating the steps you have taken to work out the situation. This will show that you did what you could and now you need assistance. Take responsibility for the part you played in causing the conflict. Make amends and the adjustment needed to progress and achieve your team's goals.

Chapter 23:
Develop excellent customer service skills

Competition in the marketplace is fierce these days. Customers have so many options at their disposal. They do not have to settle when it comes to whom they choose to do business with. That is why it is imperative that customers receive the best service they can possibly get from you and the company you work for. If they do not, it reflects directly on the company and will negatively impact the bottom line.

Think about the times when you were treated with the utmost respect, courtesy and professionalism when shopping or visiting a company for a personal service. It made you feel good about your purchase and/or caused you to believe that you received the most for your money. The opposite is also true. Think about those times when you were not treated with respect, courtesy or with professionalism, this may have caused you not to purchase from that company or even to make a formal complaint.

Beyond the Boardroom

We all have personal lives and sometimes we bring our personal issues to work. Many people make personal phone calls and will not stop the conversation when a customer or client needs to be waited on. Instead we continue our conversation as if the customer or client is not even there. What kind of message does this send to the customer? It communicates that you do not care about the customer, your job, or the company that you work for. I realize that all jobs have slow times and can be quite boring. However, when you are being paid to do a job, such as waiting on customers, you must put yourself in their shoes and give customers the kind of respect and service that you would want to receive if you were they. Also, don't keep a person who has called the company on hold too long. Take a message and tell them that the person they are calling will get back to them. Do not transfer a call from yourself to someone else unless you know for sure that the customer will be helped and not placed on hold for an indefinite period of time. You may even take a message from the customer and take their question or issue to the individual within your company who can help them. Or when transferring a call, be sure to stay on the line with the customer to ensure that they are properly connected and appropriately assisted.

Keep in mind that you make the first and lasting impression on the customer about yourself and the company you work for. If you do not like the company you work for, then do yourself and the company a favor and find a job where you'll be willing to give and do your very best.

Chapter 24:
Avoid touching in the workplace

Touching in the workplace is always risky. Avoid this unnecessary risk by keeping your touching to a firm handshake. You can never go wrong. Many times affectionate people are perceived negatively because they kiss or hug in the business environment. However, this may be misconstrued as romantic or inappropriate gestures and may make some people feel uncomfortable. In today's litigious society and due to sexual harassment issues, it is always better to lean towards caution. Many times, people become too familiar in the workplace and develop friendships where they feel comfortable enough to give a hug or kiss on the cheek. However, this behavior is unprofessional. In the workplace, avoid this temptation by focusing your energy on remembering peoples name and greeting individuals warmly with a smile and using their names whenever possible.

Again, regarding office romances, as stated in Chapter 21, these relationships need to be kept discreet and you should know and adhere to company policy. Always think about the consequences of starting an office romance. Consider such things as the relationship failing and ending on a bad note; the negative effect on your reputation; the possibility of losing your job and/or lastly, the mental and emotional anguish caused by having to work with the individual and not being able to function professionally. That said, after you've weighed all of the consequences, and this is not an illicit affair, tell your boss if it persists and you are moving towards marriage. Your company may be more willing to accommodate you if you need to transfer to a different department or if one or both of you need to relocate.

Chapter 25:
Try not to burn bridges when you leave a company

If you must terminate your employment with a company, do it professionally and with dignity. You never know if you will need to return to a company you previously worked for. Also, you never know who knows you in the new company where you want to be employed. Therefore, give your employer at least a written two-week notice before leaving the company. If you have an exceptionally good relationship with your boss, you may want to give him or her a heads-up prior to making your termination formal. However, be ready for the unexpected negative response. To play it safe, it's always better to have your termination in writing and then explain to your boss why you are leaving. Thank your boss(es) for affording you the opportunity to work in the department. Also, thank them for the knowledge and experience you acquired and their interest in your career development. Your company may be so determined to keep you that they may make a counter offer. If you want to consider the counter offer, request time to think about it. However, if you know for certain that you intend to leave, graciously decline the offer.

If on the other hand, you realize that your relationship with your boss and/or co-workers was not a good one, do your best to make amends before you leave the company. If necessary, speak to your boss's boss and explain the situation. Always have an alternate source for future references, if you know that it will not be in your best interest to use your immediate supervisor. However, regardless of the state of the relationship, you want to terminate your employment on a positive note. Much of this depends on you.

Conclusion

In conclusion, discretion is key to success in the corporate environment. Maintaining a low profile, while at the same time being known for your positive contributions, strong work ethic and pleasing personality will definitely make your life at work easier, happier and more satisfying. Also, your career goals will be more attainable. Moderation will protect your reputation and enhance your professional image in the workplace. Be sure to dress appropriately at work and during business-related events. All of this will help you to win the game in corporate America and beyond the boardroom.